PROFESSOR RAMAN PRINJA

RECIPE FOR A SOLAR SYSTEM

ILLUSTRATED BY
KRISTINA KISTER

Discover the cosmic ingredients of stars, planets, moons and more!

WAYLAND

To two amazing cooks, my mums Kushal Prinja and Tara Sharma – R. P.

For my dad Oleg and my friend Hendrik, my most favourite picky eaters – K. K.

Editor: Grace Glendinning
Designer: Aki Nakayama
Designer: Smart Design Studio
Illustrations: Kristina Kister

ISBN: 978 1 5263 2240 1 HBK
ISBN: 978 1 5263 2241 8 PBK
ISBN: 978 1 5263 2586 0 EBOOK

Printed and bound in China

SAFETY PRECAUTIONS
We recommend adult supervision at all times while doing the cooking recipes in this book. Always be aware that ingredients may contain allergens, so check the packaging for allergens if there is a risk of an allergic reaction. Anyone with a known allergy must avoid these.
• Wear an apron and cover surfaces.
• Tie back long hair.
• Ask an adult for permission and help.
• Check all ingredients for allergens.
• Clear up all spills straight away.

Wayland, an imprint of
Hachette Children's Group
Part of Hodder and Stoughton
Carmelite House
50 Victoria Embankment
London EC4Y 0DZ

An Hachette UK Company
www.hachette.co.uk
www.hachettechildrens.co.uk

The website addresses (URLs) included in this book were valid at the time of going to press. However, it is possible that contents or addresses may have changed since the publication of this book. No responsibility for any such changes can be accepted by either the author or the Publisher.

CONTENTS

INTRODUCTION

Our solar system is a brilliantly balanced group of cosmic wonders. It is made up of a fiery star, the Sun, and lots of smaller objects swirling around that central star. It is much like a big, beautiful chocolate box, glittering with an amazing variety of cosmic treats of different sizes, shapes and centres!

To make something come together from different ingredients, as our solar system has, we need some instructions – like a recipe when baking a delicious cake. This book is your step-by-step guide for how our solar system was 'cooked up'.

It's a recipe for a solar system!

DELICIOUS VARIETY

Aside from the Sun, the main objects of the solar system are:

* planets
* moons
* small rocky asteroids
* icy comets and a sprinkling of dwarf planets.

The Sun is by far the largest thing in our solar system. You could fit more than a million Earths inside a ball the size of the Sun! The huge Sun's strong gravity holds the solar system together, keeping everything from the biggest planets to the smallest rocks in circle-shaped orbits around it.

CLOUDY BEGINNING

Our solar system's many space objects started to form out of the same huge cloud of gas and dust about 4.6 billion years ago. The recipe in this book shows how.

Starting from the exploded stars that formed the gas and dust cloud in the first place, we will go through the main steps in time-order until we have the planets and moons we see today.

Here is the timeline that we will follow:

*Turn the page and start the recipe to better understand all these amazing events!

4,600 MILLION (4.6 BILLION) YEARS AGO:

A cloud of gas and dust known as a nebula starts to collapse under its own gravity. Most of this mass gathers near the centre to make the Sun.

4,590 MILLION YEARS AGO:

The nebula is now crushed into a plate-like (or disc) shape. The giant planets Jupiter, Saturn, Uranus and Neptune start to form around the very young Sun.

4,550 MILLION YEARS AGO:

The Sun begins nuclear fusion reactions and starts to shine.

4,500 MILLION YEARS AGO:

The rocky planets Mercury, Venus, Earth and Mars form. A Mars-sized planet collides with Earth to make the Moon.

4,500 TO 4,100 MILLION YEARS AGO:

A strong solar wind clears out lots of matter from the solar system.

4,100 TO 3,800 MILLION YEARS AGO:

Small rocky bodies bombard the inner planets and deliver water to Earth.

4,000 TO 3,000 MILLION YEARS AGO:

Lots of volcanoes are erupting on the inner planets.

3,800 TO 3,500 MILLION YEARS AGO:

Life begins on Earth.

3,000 MILLION YEARS AGO:

Mars loses most of its atmosphere and water.

100 MILLION YEARS AGO:

Saturn gets its rings and volcanic activity ends on the Moon.

TODAY:

The solar system is settled and is a much calmer place.

THE RAW INGREDIENTS

As with all recipes, we start with the key ingredients. To build planets and moons in a solar system, we need lots of rubble. That means we begin by gathering the chemical elements of rock, such as:

6 C CARBON	12 Mg MAGNESIUM	8 O OXYGEN	14 Si SILICON
7 N NITROGEN	26 Fe IRON		

▼ FOLLOW THE STEPS BELOW ▼

STEP 1: BANG OUT SOME HYDROGEN AND HELIUM!

Shortly after the Universe began with a Big Bang about 13.8 billion years ago, huge amounts of the elements hydrogen and helium were made.

STEP 2: SET YOUR TIMERS FOR ... MASSIVE STARS

At that point, the Universe cooled too quickly to form rubble-making ingredients, which are heavier and can only be 'cooked' inside powerful stars. But these stars won't exist for a few hundred million years!

Cooking a solar system takes some patience ...

STEP 3: HEAT YOUR STARS UNTIL THEY ARE PIPING HOT IN THE MIDDLE

Finally, deep in the centre of these enormous stars, amazing energy-making events begin – called fusion reactions – which produce the ingredients we need for our rubble.

STEP 4: ADD IN SOME GOOD SPREADING

Now that we have the chemical elements inside our stars, we need to wait again – a few million to billion years.

Set your timers for ... COSMIC FIREWORKS!

STEP 5: WATCH YOUR STARS CAREFULLY, AS THEY BURST APART

Once all the reactions are used up, the stars will become unstable as they run out of energy to support themselves. The most massive stars will explode as supernovae.

1

BIG BANG →

2

MASSIVE STARS

3

Fusion reactions in here

These early generations of stars are the ancestors of our Sun!

4

COSMIC FIREWORKS

5

Supernova!

STEP 6: SPREAD OUT THOSE KEY INGREDIENTS

The incredibly powerful supernova explosions will destroy the stars, and all the planet-making elements inside them will be launched outwards across vast distances in space.

STEP 7: RECYCLING STARDUST

The matter that we need to make our solar system comes from a whole bunch of these stars that have completed their life cycle, from birth to death.

Their deaths provide the chemical elements that combine in different ways to make different gases, minerals and tiny specks of dust (which are nearly 100 times smaller than the width of a human hair!).

Space acts like a giant cosmic recycling plant, where the ashes of dead stars and the nuclear fusion waste they leave behind are used to make new stars, planets and moons.

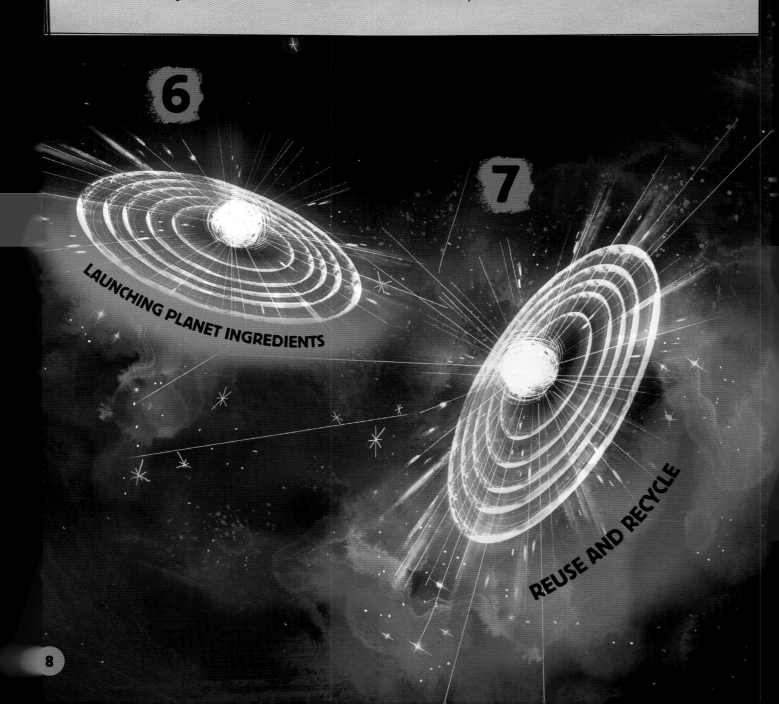

6

7

LAUNCHING PLANET INGREDIENTS

REUSE AND RECYCLE

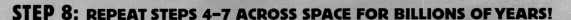

STEP 8: REPEAT STEPS 4–7 ACROSS SPACE FOR BILLIONS OF YEARS!

It can take billions of years for the right amount of supernovae explosions to scatter enough matter in space and for it to gather as a giant cloud of gas and dust called a nebula.

One such nebula, richly loaded with chemical elements from dying stars, was just about ready about 5 billion years ago …

… this is the solar nebula from which we can move to the next stage of our recipe.

OUR SOLAR NEBULA COOKING POT

The giant collection of gas and dust in a nebula is the birthplace of the Sun and planets. We now need to give the ball-like nebula a good squeeze and get it into better shape for making a solar system.

▼ ▼ ▼ **FOLLOW THE STEPS BELOW** ▼ ▼ ▼

STEP 1: PACK IT DOWN

The nebula is about 500 trillion km across – the gas and dust inside it is too loosely packed to make bodies, such as planets.

To make the matter come together, we need a **blast wave** from a nearby supernova explosion. This massive burst can help to start the collapse of the nebula.

STEP 2: SWIRL IT UP

The blast should also give the cloud a spin.

STEP 3: USE THE FORCE

The force of gravity will then help us out and squeeze the cloud further, making the gas and dust pack much closer together.

STEP 4: START THE PANCAKES

When a cloud of gas in space collapses while it is also spinning, it will always form a flattened disk, or pancake shape.

The flat gas structure is known as a proto-planetary disk, and it ends up about 1 trillion km wide.

STEP 5: SET YOUR TIMER FOR … PANCAKES!

The process from start to finish – from large ball-shaped cloud to flat disk – takes about 10 million years.

STEP 6: GATHER UP THE CENTRE

Over the next 1,000 years, matter from the proto-planetary disk is mainly pulled towards the centre by gravity. Slowly, the size and packing of the middle will grow.

This is where our star, **the Sun**, will be made using the huge amount of matter available.

SEVERAL DASHES OF PLANETESIMALS

Much like how we bake a cake starting with lots of tiny grains of ingredients, such as flour, sugar and salt, larger bodies in the solar system are assembled by first bringing together tiny bits of matter.

▼ ▼ ▼ FOLLOW THE STEPS BELOW ▼ ▼ ▼

Once the correct chemical elements, lots of gas and dust specks have drifted across space and collected in our solar nebula, we need to work to make these tiny bits join together ...

STEP 1: STIR SOME MORE UNTIL THE DUST BECOMES CLUMPS

We start with microscopic grains of dust, but as they float around the solar nebula they gently collide with one another to form larger clumps.

STEP 2: KEEP WORKING THE CLUMPS AND WATCH THEM GROW!

The clumps then combine with each other to form larger rocks.

These newly formed rocks are called **planetesimals**.

They are a key part of the history of planets and moons in our solar system.

STEP 3: KNEAD INTO PROTOPLANETS

Over millions of years, as the rocky bodies grow, their gravity becomes stronger and stronger.

Slowly the planetesimals knead together with the help of this strengthening gravity. They will grow to many kilometres across.

Once the rocky objects are about the size of the Moon, they have become what are called **protoplanets**.

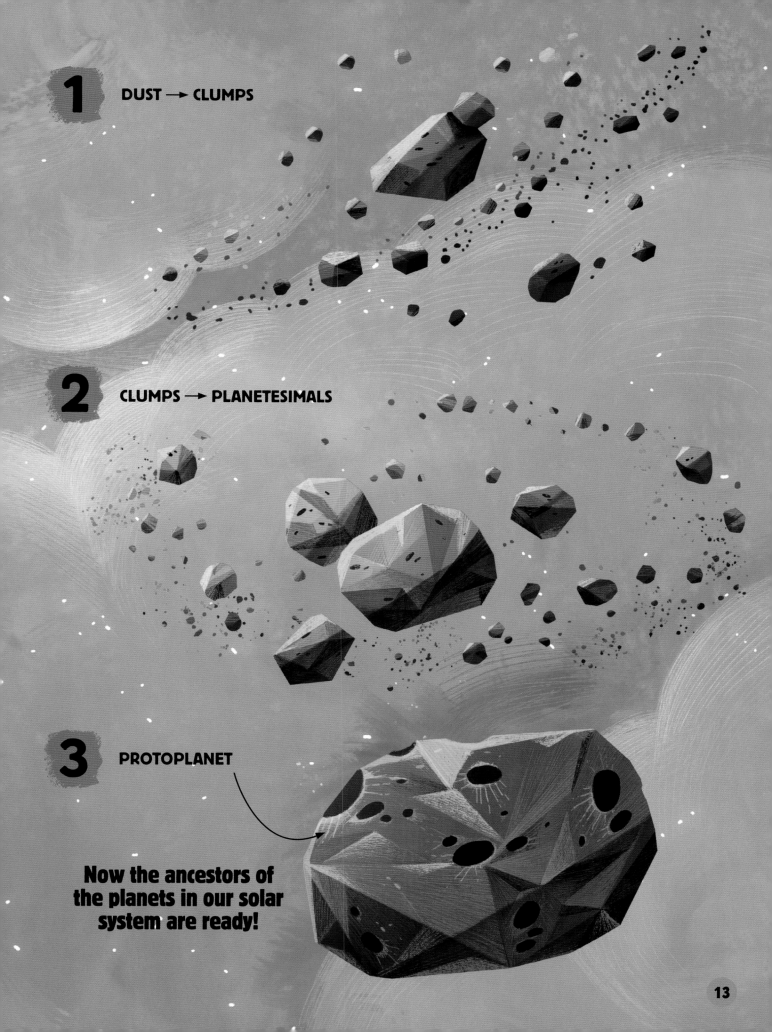

1 DUST → CLUMPS

2 CLUMPS → PLANETESIMALS

3 PROTOPLANET

Now the ancestors of the planets in our solar system are ready!

SEEDS OF THE INNER SOLAR SYSTEM

The temperature of the early solar system is very important at this point in the recipe! With the newly formed Sun turning up the heat, the inner solar system is much hotter than the outer areas.

1 HEAT TO 1,700°C

▼ ▼ ▼ FOLLOW THE STEPS BELOW ▼ ▼ ▼

STEP 1: PREHEAT THE CENTRE OF THE SOLAR SYSTEM UP TO 1,700°C

In the inner solar system, temperatures are so hot that only matter that melts at *very high* temperatures can stay solid.

So, as our protoplanets grow, parts of them will melt away from the extreme conditions. Only matter such as **iron**, **silicon**, **magnesium** and **calcium** can remain solid here.

STEP 2: GATHER THE INGREDIENTS FOR MAKING ROCKY PLANETS, LIKE OUR EARTH

The super-high temperatures mean that the ingredients for the bits of our inner solar system will be these metals that have not melted away.

Out of these ingredients, small rocky planets and asteroids can be formed.

2 SURVIVING INGREDIENTS:

IRON   SILICON   MAGNESIUM   CALCIUM

MOULDING MERCURY, VENUS, EARTH AND MARS

The ingredients of our four rocky planets need to be packed together tightly to make them nice and solid. For this part of the recipe, we're working on the four planets closest to the Sun.

▼ ▼ ▼ FOLLOW THE STEPS BELOW ▼ ▼ ▼

STEP 1: MEASURE CAREFULLY TO GET THEIR SIZES RIGHT

* Earth is the largest with a diameter of 12,742 km.
* Venus is slightly smaller than Earth, at 12,104 km across.
* Mars is just over half the diameter of Earth, which makes its diameter 6,779 km.
* Mercury, the closest planet to the Sun, is the smallest inner planet, measuring just 4,880 km across.

STEP 2: START THEM SPINNING AT VERY PARTICULAR SPEEDS!

Like spinning tops, the planets turn (or rotate) on their axis. How quickly a planet spins depends on how much spin there was in the matter that came together to make the planet in the first place.

* Earth takes just under 24 hours to spin once on its axis and we call this a day.
* Counting in Earth days, Mercury takes 58.6 days to spin once.
* Venus takes 243 Earth days to spin once.
* Mars turns once every 24.62 hours.

STEP 3: SET THEIR ORBITS JUST RIGHT

The gravity of the Sun holds these inner planets tightly together as they orbit. Planets closer to the Sun orbit faster so that they can balance against the stronger pull of gravity and not just spiral in and smash into the Sun.

Also, the closer-in they are to the Sun, the shorter their lap distance! The time it takes a planet to complete one lap or orbit is known as a year.

* For Earth, a year is just over 365 days.
* A year on Mercury is only 88 Earth days.
* Venus's year is 225 Earth days.
* Mars has the longest year, at 687 Earth days.

SEEDS OF THE OUTER SOLAR SYSTEM

Much further away from the young Sun, the outer solar system stays a lot cooler. We must bake the planets out here at very different temperatures!

▼ ▼ ▼ FOLLOW THE STEPS BELOW ▼ ▼ ▼

STEP 1: COOL THE OUTER SOLAR SYSTEM TO -100°C AND ADD ICE!

At about 700 million km from the Sun, temperatures will drop below an incredibly cold -100ºC, to form many types of ice. Along with water ice, there are also ices made of carbon dioxide and methane.

At this point in our recipe, there is a lot of this type of matter available in the outer solar system, so the planets can gradually grow into giant, gaseous worlds.

Gathering up four giant planets

STEP 2: STICK IT ALL TOGETHER

The icy material in the cold outer solar system acts like a glue to gather up rocky matter and stick it together to make very large objects.

Solid bodies of around 10 times the mass of Earth come together, which form the solid inner cores of the four giant planets.

STEP 3: ADD LAYERS OF LEFTOVER GASES

The strong gravity of these huge cores pulls in lots of the leftover gases from the early days of the Universe – hydrogen and helium – to form the enormous atmospheres of the giant gas planets: Jupiter, Saturn, Uranus and Neptune.

STEP 4: MEASURE OUT JUST THE RIGHT AMOUNT OF MASS FOR EACH PLANET

- ❈ Jupiter pulls in so much mass that it reaches 318 times the mass of Earth.
- ❈ Saturn has 95 Earth masses.
- ❈ Uranus has 14.5 Earth masses.
- ❈ Neptune is 17 times more massive than Earth.

STEP 5: GIVE EACH PLANET A REALLY GOOD SPIN

Gas giant planets all spin very fast.

- ❈ Jupiter takes just nine Earth hours and 51 Earth minutes to spin once on its axis.
- ❈ Saturn spins once in 10 hours and 42 minutes.
- ❈ Neptune is 16 hours and six minutes.
- ❈ Uranus spins the slowest, taking 17 hours and 14 minutes to turn once.

STEP 6: FINALLY, GET THOSE ORBITS ON TRACK

The far-out giant planets have enormously long orbits around the Sun.

- ❈ Jupiter takes 12 Earth years to complete a lap.
- ❈ Saturn takes 29 Earth years to lap the Sun.
- ❈ Uranus takes 84 Earth years to orbit.
- ❈ Neptune takes 164.8 Earth years.

1 COOL TO -100°C

2 GATHER THE CORE

3 GAS ALL AROUND

4 EARTH X 318 — JUPITER
EARTH X 95 — SATURN
EARTH X 14.5 — URANUS
EARTH X 17 — NEPTUNE

5 FASTEST
SLOWER
SLOWEST
SECOND SLOWEST

6 JUPITER
SATURN
URANUS
NEPTUNE

19

SOLAR WIND CAST-OFF

Let's check in on the Sun, as it continues to heat up in the middle. It is growing and powering up, and it's about to have a big impact on the rest of our solar system recipe.

1

STEP 1: SEND OUT A BLAST OF WIND ACROSS THE SOLAR SYSTEM

When a star powers up with nuclear reactions at its core, there is a huge energy release, which sends out a strong solar wind.

This wind is actually a flow of particles, such as protons and electrons, streaming away from the Sun. It is travelling across the solar system and sweeping most bits of gas and dust from the nebula deep into space.

STEP 2: SET ASIDE THE FINISHED PLANETS (FOR NOW)

The Sun's forceful cast-off of most of the remaining bits of matter in the solar system ends the planet-making phase in the recipe of our solar system.

STEP 3: KEEP THE WINDS BLOWING TO SEE STUNNING COLOURS IN THE SKY

Today, billions of years later, the Sun still has a – much weaker – solar wind. It carries electrically charged particles and magnetic clouds of gas in all directions away from the Sun. Sometimes this flow strikes our planet, at speeds of a million km per hour.

The particles collide with atoms in Earth's atmosphere, giving them energy to release as light. We sometimes see this light as beautiful shimmering patterns of colour in the sky known as the **Northern and Southern lights** (or aurorae).

AURORAE

LEFTOVERS

When we cook things, there are often some ingredients left over to make yourself a bit of something extra. In a similar way, even after the Sun and planets form, and the solar winds pass through, bits of dust and rocks remain in the solar system. We now know these as the many millions of asteroids and icy comets still swarming around today.

1 ASTEROID BELT

STEP 1: PLACE THE 'LEFTOVER ASTEROIDS' MOSTLY BETWEEN JUPITER AND MARS

This area is known as the **asteroid belt**. The asteroids will range in size from several hundred km across to chunky lumps less than 1 km wide.

STEP 2: NEXT, SCATTER SOME OF THESE LEFTOVERS, BUT BE CAREFUL WHERE THEY LAND!

Sometimes asteroids can crash into each other and be sent hurtling out of the asteroid belt and towards the Sun.

Some of them may even come close enough to Earth and get caught by its gravity. Then our leftovers get new names!

They may enter our planet's atmosphere as **meteors**, which can be seen as streaking lights in the night sky.

Those that survive the scorching heat of passing through the atmosphere and strike the ground are known as **meteorites**.

LEFTOVERS ARE ALSO GREAT FROZEN!

STEP 3:
Place some of your leftovers way out in the enormous ball-shaped area circling the outer the solar system, called the Oort cloud, and mix them up with ice, forming dirty snowball-like **comets**.

STEP 4: SEND SOME OF YOUR FROZEN LEFTOVERS INTO ORBIT FOR A BEAUTIFUL SHOW!

When a comet gets knocked out of the Oort cloud and heads on a trip around the Sun, it heats up and spews out dust and gases, which form a tail stretching millions of kilometres away from the Sun.

From Earth, it is a stunning sight in the night sky.

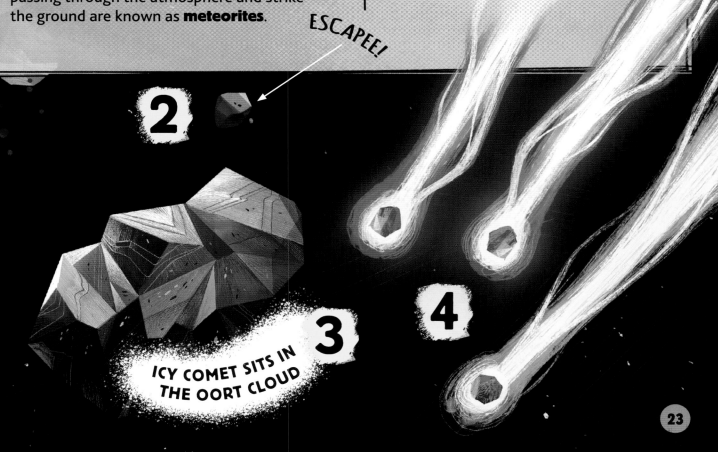

ESCAPEE!

2

3 ICY COMET SITS IN THE OORT CLOUD

4

DWARF PLANET SPRINKLING

DWARF SPRINKLES

Along with making the eight main planets, billions of asteroids and comets, and a variety of moons, there are *still* ingredients in the solar nebula to make some other larger bodies known as dwarf planets.

The dwarf planets aren't considered full planets because they are smaller, and so don't have strong enough gravity to clear their orbits around the Sun of other rocks and debris.

▼ ▼ ▼ FOLLOW THE STEPS BELOW ▼ ▼ ▼

STEP 1: MAKE A BATCH OF FIVE DWARF PLANETS

We know of at least five dwarf planets sprinkled across our solar system.

✳ The closest to Earth is Ceres, which lies in the asteroid belt between Mars and Jupiter.

✳ Pluto is the most famous dwarf planet. With a diameter of 2,377 km, it is also the largest.

✳ Haumea has a strange egg-like appearance and it spins so fast that its day is just four hours long.

✳ Eris is the furthest dwarf planet from the Sun. It is located beyond the orbit of Neptune and takes 558 years to complete just one lap around the Sun.

✳ Makemake is a bit smaller than Pluto, and even has its own tiny moon!

Over billions of years, as the solar system settles down, the dwarf planets will change much less than the main planets. Their frozen surfaces today have locked in the conditions from a time when the solar system was very young.

ERIS

CLOSE -UP!

ERIS HAS **LOTS** OF METHANE ICE!

PLUTO HAS A ♥-SHAPED SEA!

HAUMEA HAS A RING! ↗

MAKEMAKE HAS A REDDISH SURFACE

CERES LOOKS VERY SIMILAR TO THE MOON!

MAKEMAKE

PLUTO

HAUMEA

CERES

LAYERED PLANETS

Just as cakes can have several layers of different ingredients and textures, the next stages of the recipe for our four rocky inner planets includes lots of layers!

1

HEAVIER

2

CRUST

MANTLE

INNER CORE

OUTER CORE

▼ ▼ ▼ CRAFTING THE LAYERS ▼ ▼ ▼

As we saw on pages 14–15 of our solar system recipe, when the planets first formed, they were so hot that most of their rock and metal melted as a liquid. This is the beginning of the layering process.

STEP 1: SEPARATE EACH ELEMENT ACCORDING TO ITS WEIGHT

Slowly, to begin forming our layers, the heaviest ingredients, such as pure metal, will sink to the centre or core. The lighter matter, such as aluminium and silicon, will float to the upper layers and cool down.

STEP 2: START BUILDING UP EARTH'S AMAZING AND COMPLEX FOUR MAIN LAYERS

The top layer is the one we live on and is called the crust. It is between 8 km to 50 km thick.

The next layer down is the mantle, which is made of rocks and minerals. Since the inside of Earth remains very hot, the mantle material is molten. It is 3,000 km thick and moves around a bit like treacle.

Below the mantle is Earth's core, made of iron and nickel metal. The core has two parts.

There's a liquid outer core and beneath that, an inner core, which is 6,000°C hot but is tightly squashed into a solid ball of metal.

STEP 3: PREPARE ALL REMAINING LAYERS

Venus is thought to have similar inside layers to Earth, so repeat the above steps here.

Though Mercury is the smallest rocky planet, it has the largest core making up 85% of the planet's interior. Be sure to measure carefully!

And finally, along with its layers of mantle and surface crust, Mars has a mostly solid core.

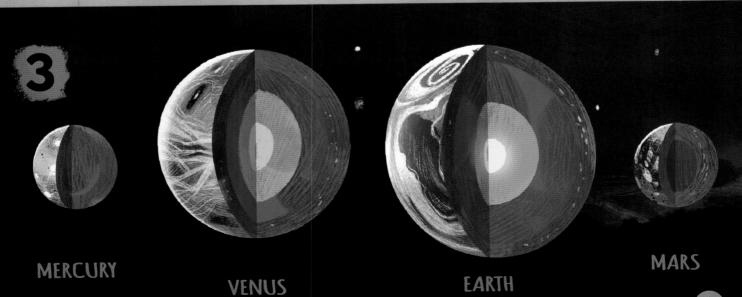

3

MERCURY

VENUS

EARTH

MARS

FORMING THE GIANT FOUR

The insides of the four giant gas planets in the outer solar system also have layers. But they don't have a hard surface you can stand on. To make these planets, we must carefully measure how hot their insides are and apply an enormous amount of pressure.

▼ ▼ ▼ FOLLOW THE STEPS BELOW ▼ ▼ ▼

STEP 1: START WITH YOUR TWO BIGGEST GIANTS

✳ Jupiter and Saturn will need large cores of rock and metal that can be as hot as 15,000°C.

✳ Above the core they must have layers of metallic hydrogen and liquid hydrogen added.

✳ Above the hydrogen layers, we place a gassy atmosphere of mainly hydrogen and helium, which is topped with clouds of water and ammonia ice.

STEP 2: MOVE ON TO THE SMALLER TWO

✳ Uranus and Neptune are the smaller of the four gas planets and are further from the Sun than Jupiter and Saturn.

✳ They must also have cores of rock and metal, surrounded by an extremely hot fluid that's a mixture of water, ammonia and methane.

✳ Uranus and Neptune will also need upper atmosphere layers of hydrogen, helium and methane gas. The methane in this area gives these two planets a beautiful blue colour.

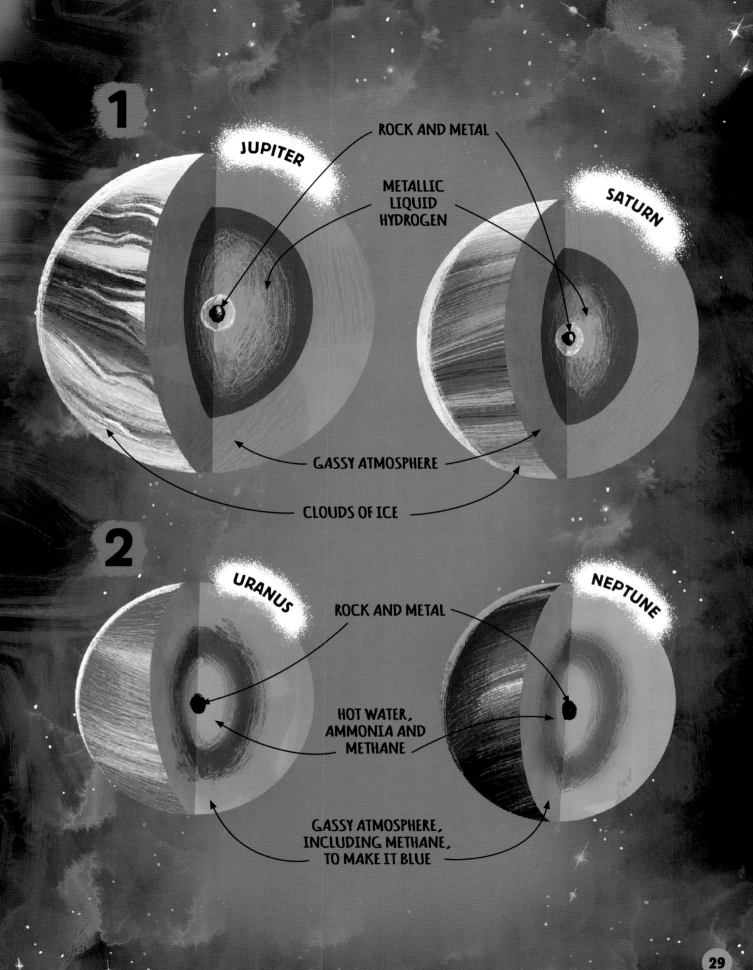

1

JUPITER

ROCK AND METAL

METALLIC LIQUID HYDROGEN

SATURN

GASSY ATMOSPHERE

CLOUDS OF ICE

2

URANUS

ROCK AND METAL

NEPTUNE

HOT WATER, AMMONIA AND METHANE

GASSY ATMOSPHERE, INCLUDING METHANE, TO MAKE IT BLUE

A COSMIC BASHING

It's time to get a bit messy, as the solar system at this stage is still a really dangerous place. Even a billion years after the planets form, their orbits are littered with swarming space rocks, which have not settled into orbits.

This makes the solar system a violent shooting gallery! This part of the recipe involves some big rocks colliding with the planets, sometimes causing very big changes.

✳ ✳ ✳ IT'S BOMBARDMENT TIME ✳ ✳ ✳

STEP 1: KNOCK OVER URANUS

Some kind of flying cosmic body with at least twice the mass of Earth will need to slam into the young planet Uranus and knock it over!

So, while all the other planets spin upright in their orbits around the Sun, Uranus is tilted over by almost a right angle. It is set to roll around the Sun like a barrel.

STEP 2: MAKE SOME CRATERS

We must also form the bowl-shaped scars, or craters, decorating the rocky planets and moons. These features form when asteroids and other lumps of matter smash into the surfaces of the planets and dig out chunks of material.

STEP 3: JUST ADD WATER

Icy asteroids and comets are also the water bearers of our solar system recipe. It is likely that the huge amount of asteroids that crashed into Earth billions of years ago delivered the first water to our planet.

Today, 70% of Earth's surface is covered in oceans and lakes. This liquid water was very important in getting life started on Earth.

1

URANUS

2

CRATERS

Bodies, such as Mercury, that have no winds or weather to wear them away, have numerous impact craters still visible today.

3

WATER DELIVERY

SMASHING TOGETHER A MOON

Earth and the Moon are a very special pairing in the overall recipe of the solar system.

✷ ✷ ✷ RECIPE FOR A VERY SPECIAL RELATIONSHIP ✷ ✷ ✷

STEP 1: WAIT FOR JUST THE RIGHT MOMENT

After the Sun comes to life as a blazing star, and planets begin to form, we must wait about another 150 million years before Earth gains a moon.

STEP 2: PREPARE FOR A BIG COLLISION!

The violent smashes during these early times of the solar system are likely responsible for building Earth's moon. At this stage of the recipe, a body about the size of Mars careers at great speed into the inner solar system.

It collides with Earth and throws huge chunks of Earth's crust into space. Gravity brings together the ejected material and it gradually forms the ball-shaped body that becomes the Moon.

This is why Earth and the Moon are made up of very similar material.

STEP 3: GET THE SIZE AND SHAPE RIGHT FOR A BEAUTIFULLY BALANCED RELATIONSHIP

At a quarter of the diameter of Earth, the Moon is very large compared to the size of its host planet. No other planet in the solar system has a moon that is so large compared to its own size.

The Moon orbits Earth once per month, as the pair journey together around the Sun. All the time, the Moon's gravity tugs on Earth's oceans to make tides.

1 WAIT 150 MILLION YEARS

MOON MOMENT

2

DEBRIS IN ORBIT

MOON FORMATION

COLLISION

3

THE TIDAL PULL

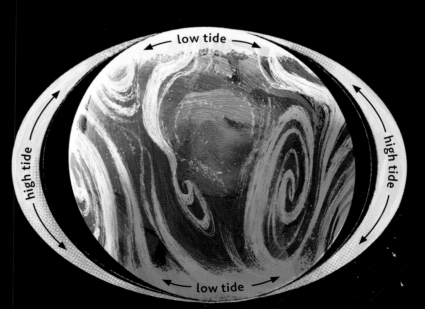

low tide

high tide

high tide

low tide

A BIG BATCH OF MOONS

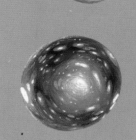

An important addition to our solar system recipe is a mixture of moons. Earth has one moon, but there are at least 200 more in our solar system.

Sometimes called 'natural satellites', the moons come in many shapes, sizes and types. A few of them even have atmospheres of their own or oceans beneath their surfaces!

✳ INGREDIENTS NEEDED FOR A DIVERSE BATCH OF MOONS ✳

GAS AND DUST: As we have just seen, Earth's moon formed from a giant collision but most of the other moons will be assembled out of the gas and dust that circled as the planets themselves were being made.

STOLEN MOONS: The giant gas planets in particular, with their strong gravity, are also able to capture moons that formed elsewhere but stray close to these large worlds.

INNER BATCH: Out of the rocky (or terrestrial) planets in the inner solar system, Mercury and Venus do not have moons. And aside from Earth's one moon, Mars has two tiny moons barely 10 km across, called Deimos and Phobos.

OUTER BATCH: This is where it gets interesting!

The giant planet Jupiter has 79 moons, some with amazing features.

Its moon Io has active volcanoes, while Europa is thought to have vast oceans of salty water beneath its surface. With a diameter greater than Mercury, Jupiter's moon Ganymede is the largest in the solar system.

Saturn has 82 known moons that range in size from Mercury-sized to the length of a football pitch. Its moon Enceladus erupts volcanoes of icy water. Titan, Saturn's largest moon, has a thick atmosphere and oily lakes on its surface.

Uranus has 27 moons and Neptune has 14, including Triton, which has a surface of liquid nitrogen.

MARS

JUPITER

PLUTO

SATURN

A HANDFUL OF BABY MOONS:
The dwarf planets also have moons, including five tiny ones orbiting Pluto. Haumea has a couple of moons and Eris has one. Even a few asteroids have been found to have very small moons!

URANUS

NEPTUNE

ICING AROUND THE PLANETS

There are some more decorations to add around the planets. Let's get creative with some ring-making! The four giant gas planets, Jupiter, Saturn, Uranus and Neptune, have rings around them. There are a couple of ways to make the rings.

 ## NOW START PLACING RINGS AROUND THE PLANETS

STEP 1: START WITH THE BIGGEST AND BEST

Give Saturn a beautiful, bright collection of 12 rings, made up of billions of chunks of ice and rock. The rings of Saturn are the most magnificent of any in the solar system.

End-to-end the rings stretch 273,600 km wide, but only 10 m thick. If you imagine Saturn shrunk down to the size of a basketball, then its rings would be much thinner than a human hair!

STEP 2: THEN DO ALL THE REST

Jupiter will have a set of four rings, mainly made of dust, appearing dark and faint.

Give Neptune six rings, also made from very dark, dusty material.

Uranus' set of 13 rings are the type made from a broken-up moon, forming a swarm of particles around the planet.

It is possible that other small bodies in the solar system also have very thin, dark rings. Crashes between asteroids of different sizes can leave leftovers of the smashed smaller rock circling as rings around the surviving larger asteroid.

SATURN'S RINGS

1

OPTION 1

Firstly, some bits of dust and gas that make up the planet remains too far away from the planet's core and cannot be squashed together by gravity. This material remains behind to make rings instead.

OPTION 2

In other cases, some of the moons of the giant gas planets drift in too close and get smashed up by the planet's strong gravity. The debris left behind spreads out to make rings.

NEPTUNE'S RINGS

URANUS' RINGS

JUPITER'S RINGS

ALLOW TO COOL

When you take a cake out of the oven, it slowly cools. The rocky planets also started out very hot and over billions of years they have cooled. Our solar system is almost ready now, but we can still add a few more touches to shape the planets and moons. As they all cool down, some interesting events start happening ...

▼ ▼ ▼ FOLLOW THE STEPS BELOW ▼ ▼ ▼

STEP 1: COOL A BIT TO CAUSE ERUPTIONS!

✳ Volcanoes form as a planet or moon cools down inside. A volcano is a gap in the surface layer (crust) through which molten rock called magma can pour out, along with gases, which enter the atmosphere.

✳ Magma that reaches the surface is called lava.

✳ As the lava flows, it cools down and hardens to change the shape of the rocky surface.

STEP 2: COOL FURTHER TO HARDEN

✳ Once the layers below the surface crust cool a lot, they become solid and the planet will no longer have live or active volcanoes.

✳ Volcanoes on the Moon probably last erupted during an age almost 100 million years ago when dinosaurs roamed Earth!

✳ Mars' majestic mountain called Olympus Mons is the tallest volcano in the solar system. No longer active, Olympus Mons has a height of 22 km, which is almost three times that of Earth's highest mountain, Mount Everest.

✳ Venus has more than 1,700 dead volcanic features on its surface. The planet is covered by huge lava flows that only stopped erupting a few 100 million years ago.

STEP 3: KEEP SOME LAVA FLOWING

Larger planets like Earth still have hot interiors and so still have active volcanoes today.

Jupiter's moon Io is the most volcanically active object in the solar system today. It is shooting plumes of magma and gas hundreds of kilometres above its surface. The entire surface of Io is covered with volcanoes and lava flows, giving it a pizza-like appearance!

1 ERUPTIONS!

2 OLYMPUS MONS

VENUS VOLCANO

3 KEEP THE LAVA FLOWING ON EARTH

The larger the rocky planet, the slower it cools. That's similar to how a larger glass of hot water will cool slower than a small glass.

SOME FINAL SHAKES

Quakes, shakes and tremors can also give the surfaces of rocky planets some final features. There are millions of earthquakes on our planet every year, but thankfully most of them are too small and weak to be felt by us.

✳ ✳ ✳ RECIPE FOR QUAKES ON EARTH ✳ ✳ ✳

STEP 1: SET UP THE PLATES

Earth is unique among the planets in that its outer surface is divided into several plates. Move these plates around and earthquakes will occur when the plates come together, split apart or slide against each other.

STEP 2: CREATE NEW SHAPES ON EARTH

✳ TRENCHES: When two plates on Earth collide and one moves beneath the other, deep trenches can be formed.

✳ ISLANDS AND MOUNTAINS: Plates that push up against each other can create volcanic islands and mountain ranges.

✳ NEW CRUST: If the plates pull apart from each other, magma can rise up from deep within Earth and erupt through the gap to form a new crust layer.

1 PLATES COME TOGETHER

2 EVER-CHANGING EARTH

✳ ✳ RECIPE FOR QUAKES IN THE REST OF THE SOLAR SYSTEM ✳ ✳

Though the other rocky planets don't have plates that shift around, they do still have their own quakes.

STEP 1: MAKE WRINKLES ON MERCURY

Mercury is shrinking very slightly and this makes its surface crust shrivel, like the skin of a raisin. The shrivel makes rocks push together and thrust upwards.

STEP 2: TURN UP TO EXTREME TEMPERATURES ON THE MOON

Earth's moon also has quakes, some of which are due to big temperature changes between the day and extremely cold night there. This makes the rocky material expand and contract.

STEP 3: SET UP A TUG-OF-WAR BETWEEN MARS AND ONE OF ITS MOONS, PHOBOS

Hundreds of quakes have been detected by spacecraft on Mars. A few of these are due to tugs from the gravity of its moon, Phobos. The strength of the Martian quakes is between those felt on Earth and those on the Moon.

1 WRINKLY MERCURY

2 SHIFTING MOON

3 MARS V. PHOBOS

MORE SOLAR SYSTEM RECIPES?

Our solar system recipe is now complete. Following all the steps, over billions of years, creates an amazing collection of planets, moons, asteroids, comets and dwarf planets.

The whole swarm is held together in orbits by the enormous gravity of our star, the Sun, at the very centre of the system.

However, we know of almost 5,000 other planets that are orbiting around other stars in our Milky Way Galaxy. And there are likely billions more out there waiting to be discovered!

These planets beyond our solar system are called exoplanets. Some of them are very unique and not like anything seen in our solar system. You'll need a different recipe make them!

GAS UP CLOSE

There are gas exoplanets half the mass of Jupiter orbiting their star as close as Mercury is to our Sun. (In our recipe, giant gas planets are found well away from the Sun, in the outer solar system.)

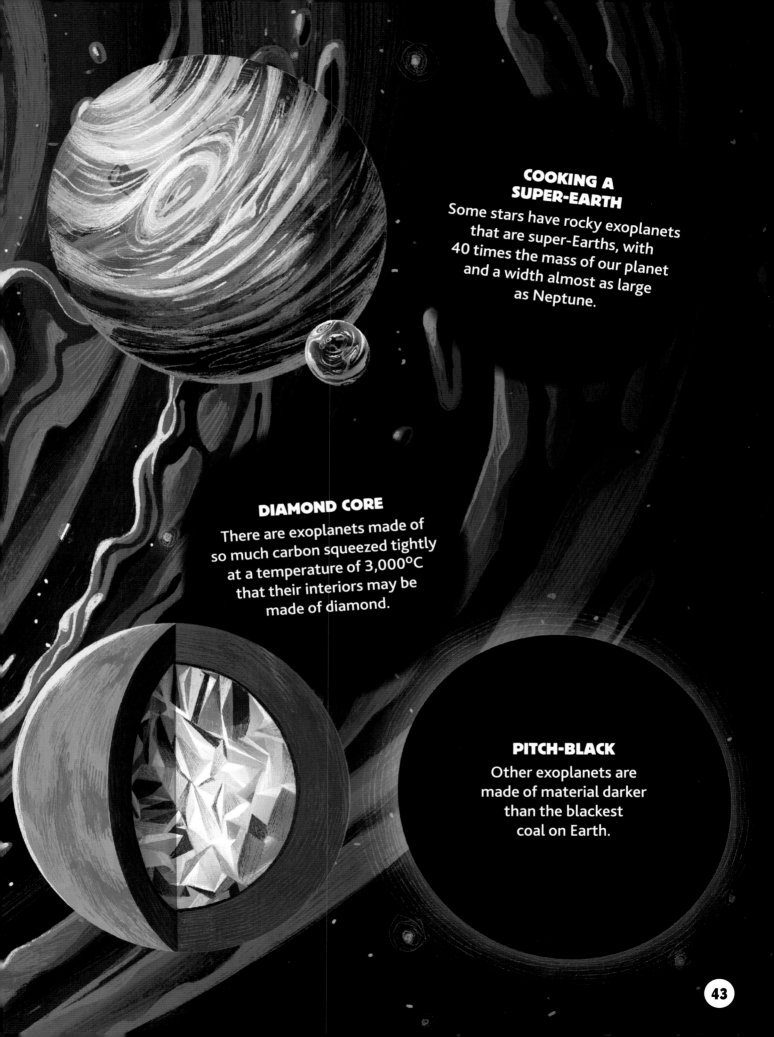

COOKING A SUPER-EARTH

Some stars have rocky exoplanets that are super-Earths, with 40 times the mass of our planet and a width almost as large as Neptune.

DIAMOND CORE

There are exoplanets made of so much carbon squeezed tightly at a temperature of 3,000°C that their interiors may be made of diamond.

PITCH-BLACK

Other exoplanets are made of material darker than the blackest coal on Earth.

GREAT SOLAR SYSTEM BAKING CHALLENGE!

ICED PLANET BISCUITS

Finally, here are some space-themed baking suggestions for you to try with an adult. They are a delicious and fun way to enjoy the solar system!

WARNING: All cooking to be done with adult permission and supervision.
If you have any allergies to the ingredients, do not use them.

✱ ✱ ✱ RECIPE FOR ICED PLANET BISCUITS ✱ ✱ ✱

INGREDIENTS

- ✱ 100 g butter
- ✱ 100 g golden caster sugar
- ✱ 1 egg, lightly beaten
- ✱ 1 tsp vanilla extract
- ✱ 280 g plain flour, plus extra for dusting
- ✱ 250 g icing sugar
- ✱ Food colouring in various colours: red, blue, green, yellow, orange, black, brown (or you can use caramel for the brown!)

METHODS

1. Heat oven to 190°C/170°C fan/gas 5.
2. Line a baking sheet with baking paper.
3. Beat the butter and sugar together in a large mixing bowl until pale and fluffy.
4. Slowly beat in the egg and vanilla extract.
5. Stir in the flour until it comes together to form a dough.
6. On a floured surface, roll out the dough to about 3 mm thick.
7. Using round biscuit cutters of different sizes, cut a variety of biscuits between 8 cm and 3 cm wide (for different planets).
8. Place the biscuits on the baking sheet and bake for 10–12 mins until pale golden brown.
9. Leave them on the baking sheet for 5 mins, then transfer to a rack to cool.
10. Mix the icing sugar with 1 tablespoon of water, divide it into several small bowls and add food colouring to make spreadable icing for different planets:

   ❄ light blue for Uranus
   ❄ blue, green and brown for Earth
   ❄ orange for Venus
   ❄ red for Mars
   ❄ red, brown and white to make bands for Jupiter.

Munch away on your planets!

45

MOON ROCK MUNCHIES

✳ ✳ ✳ RECIPE FOR MOON ROCK MUNCHIES ✳ ✳ ✳

INGREDIENTS

✳ **400 g milk chocolate, roughly chopped (or chocolate buttons/chips)**

✳ **375 g plain popcorn**

✳ **60 g small marshmallows, cut in half**

✳ **65 g unsalted roasted peanuts (optional)**

✳ **Your favourite sprinkles**

METHODS

1. Line a mini muffin tray with mini muffin cases.

2. Very gradually melt 200 g of the chocolate in a microwave-safe bowl or a double-boiler, stirring well throughout . **Only heat until about three-quarters of the chocolate has melted. You do not want burnt chocolate!**

3. Combine the melted chocolate with the popcorn, marshmallows, remaining (unmelted) chocolate chunks and peanuts (optional).

4. Spoon the mixture into the cases.

5. Scatter with sprinkles (and maybe even some icing sugar as moon dust).

6. Allow to set at room temperature. When they are cool and solidified ...

... munch away on your Moon rocks!

WARNING: All cooking to be done with adult permission and supervision. If you have any allergies to the ingredients, do not use them.

GLOSSARY

Atmosphere The layer of gases that surround a planet.

Atom The smallest particle of a chemical element.

Axis An imaginary straight line through the centre of an object, around which the object turns.

Chemical element A basic building block of life.

Comet An object made of dust and ice, which orbits the Sun.

Cosmic body Asteroids, comets, meteors and planets are all cosmic bodies.

Dwarf planet An object in space, smaller than a planet, that rotates around the Sun.

Electron One of the three particles in an atom.

Gravity The force of attraction between two objects. Gravity on Earth pulls us down and makes objects fall to the ground. Gravity in space keeps all the planets in orbit around the Sun.

Mass The amount of matter in an object.

Matter The stuff that things are made of – anything that takes up space is called matter.

Nebula A loose cloud of gas and dust in which a star is born.

Neutron One of the three particles in an atom.

Nuclear fusion Stars get their energy from nuclear fusion. This is when the lighter centres (nuclei) of two atoms join to form one or more heavier ones. This process releases enormous amounts of energy.

Orbit The curved path of a planet or other object as it moves around another planet, star or moon.

Particle A very small piece of something.

Plate (or tectonic plate) One of the very large pieces of rock that form Earth's crust.

Proton One of the three particles in an atom.

Solar system The Sun and all the planets, comets and other space bodies that revolve around it.

Star A ball of gases held together by its own gravity.

Supernova A particular type of star explosion.

Universe Space and everything in it.

INDEX

FURTHER READING

Wonders of the Night Sky by Professor Raman Prinja, illustrated by Jan Bielecki, Wayland 2022

The Future of the Universe by Professor Raman Prinja, illustrated by Jan Bielecki, Wayland 2022